'Vivid illustrations and wonderful poetry.'

Adrian Bethune, author of *Wellbeing In The Primary Classroom*

What if All the Trees Blow Away?

This captivating, storybook helps young people identify and explore feelings of anxiety, fear and uncertainty. As the narrator anxiously pours out a plethora of 'What if?' thoughts ranging from realistic to fantastical, these seemingly never-ending worries eventually build into what some readers may recognise as a panic attack. They discover that beneath the head full of worries lies the feeling of fear, and rather than resolving all the anxious questions, they can acknowledge and be with the fear itself.

Sensitively written and highly relatable to anyone who has experienced anxious thinking, *What if All the Trees Blow Away?*:

- has a gender-neutral central character
- helps children recognise their anxious thoughts as fear
- guides children on how to take back control of their anxious thinking
- explores the connection between emotional, mental, and physical wellbeing
- aids in normalising the feelings of fear and worry
- encourages sharing and seeking support
- ends with a mindful reflection, to help children explore and be with their feelings.

This storybook is essential reading for teachers, parents, or anyone working with children, who wishes to enable open conversations, exploration and expression around fear and anxiety.

Anita Kate Garai is a freelance teacher, writer and wellbeing consultant.

What if All the Trees Blow Away?

Exploring Anxiety, Fear and Uncertainty

Anita Kate Garai

Illustrated by Pip Williams

Routledge
Taylor & Francis Group

LONDON AND NEW YORK

Cover illustration credit: © Pip Williams

Logo and 'bubbles' design © 2022 Liz Tui Morris, www.bolster.co.nz

First published 2023
by Routledge
4 Park Square, Milton Park, Abingdon, Oxon OX14 4RN

and by Routledge
605 Third Avenue, New York, NY 10158

Routledge is an imprint of the Taylor & Francis Group, an informa business

British Library Cataloguing-in-Publication Data
A catalogue record for this book is available from the British Library

Library of Congress Cataloging-in-Publication Data
Names: Garai, Anita Kate, author. | Williams, Pip (Illustrator), illustrator.
Title: What if all the trees blow away? : exploring anxiety, fear and uncertainty / Anita Kate Garai ; illustrated by Pip Williams.
Description: Milton Park, Abingdon, Oxon ; New York, NY : Routledge, 2022.
Identifiers: LCCN 2021051864 (print) | LCCN 2021051865 (ebook) | ISBN 9781032233994 (paperback) | ISBN 9781003280163 (ebook)
Subjects: LCSH: Anxiety in children—Juvenile literature. | Worry in children—Juvenile literature. | Fear in children—Juvenile literature.
Classification: LCC BF723.A5 G37 2022 (print) | LCC BF723.A5 (ebook) | DDC 155.4/1246—dc23/eng/20220121
LC record available at https://lccn.loc.gov/2021051864
LC ebookrecord available at https://lccn.loc.gov/2021051865

ISBN: 978-1-032-23399-4 (pbk)

ISBN: 978-1-003-28016-3 (ebk)

DOI: 10.4324/9781003280163

Typeset in Londrina
by Apex CoVantage, LLC

For beautiful Raewyn and little Ani – with all our heart.

I was a child who worried A LOT.

What if it's cold?
What if it's hot?

What if the sun is too hot

and I sweat?

What if
it rains
and
I
get

really

wet?

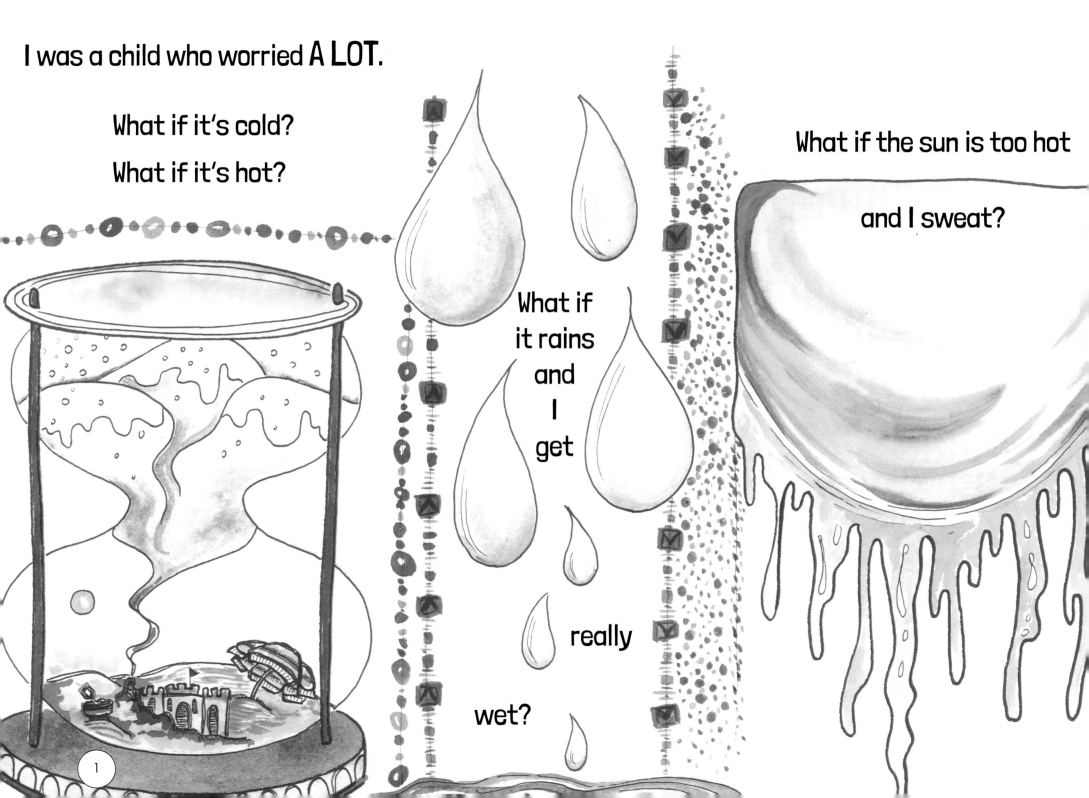

1

What if a hurricane comes one day

and all the trees just blow away?

What if the birds
from far and near

lose their way and
disappear?

What if the flowers lose their smell

and the rainbows lose their colours as well?

What if the sun forgets to rise?

What

if I can't

believe

my eyes?

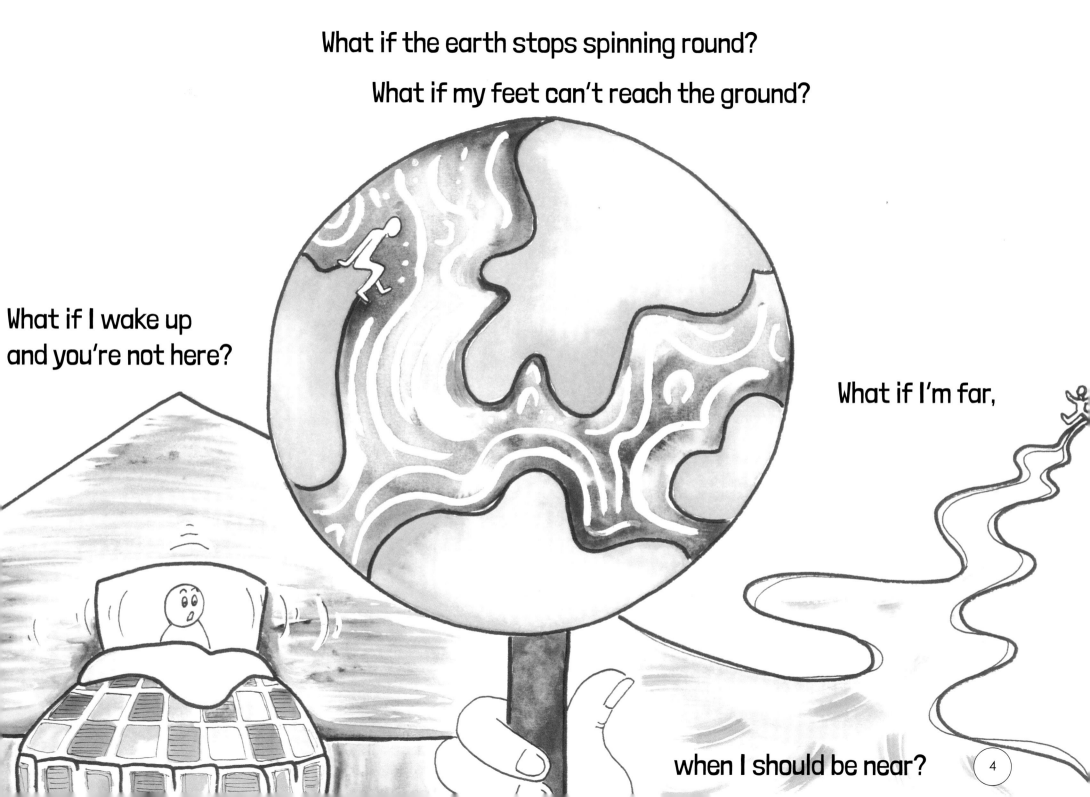

What if the fish

all swim the wrong way?

What if I get sick one day?

What if the lions lose their roar?

What if my teacher moves in next door?

(YIKES!)

5

What if we don't have
food to eat

and sugar turns sour
and salt becomes sweet?

What if I don't make any friends?

What if one day the world just . . .

ends?

What if my fingernails
all turn blue?

What if I run out of
things to do?

What if it's day when it
should be night?

What if I'm wrong
when I know I'm right?

What if the stars forget how to shine?

What if it's yours
when I *swear* it was mine?

What if I try but I'm not very good?

What if the rivers
don't flow as they should?

10

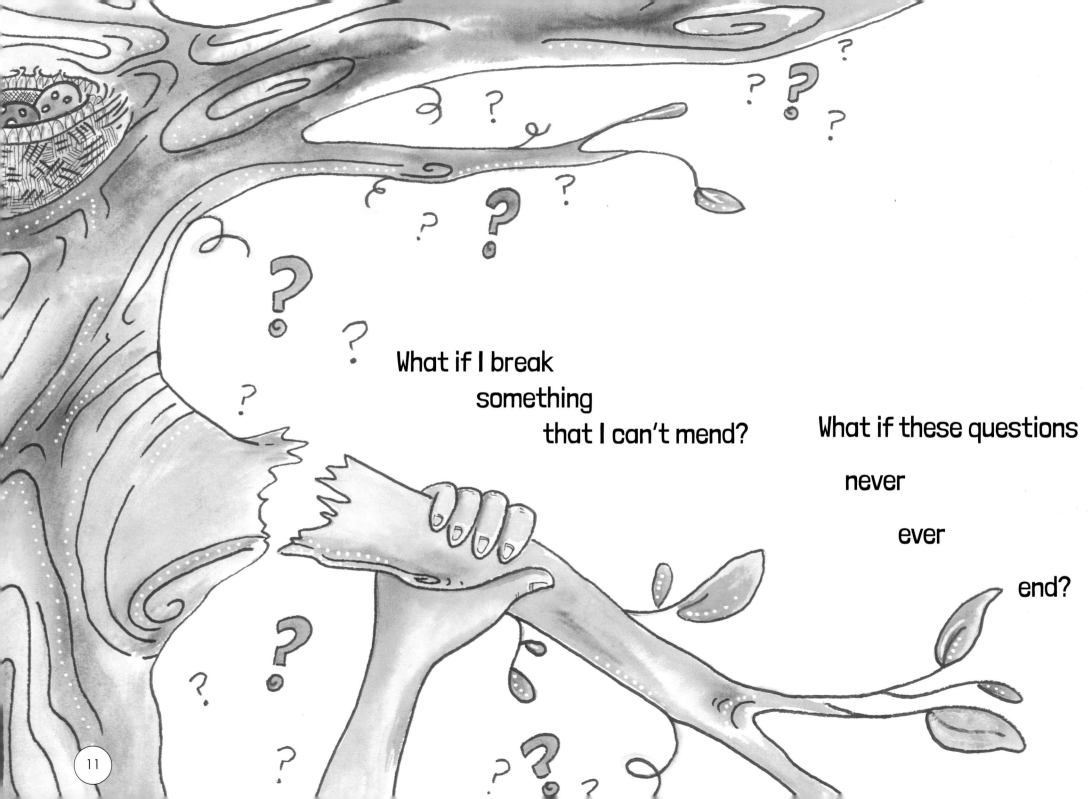

What if I break
something
that I can't mend?

What if these questions

never

ever

end?

11

Then one day

I felt something tight in my belly

and my legs began to feel rather like jelly.

And next I could feel a trembling start.

It rose from my tummy right up to my heart.

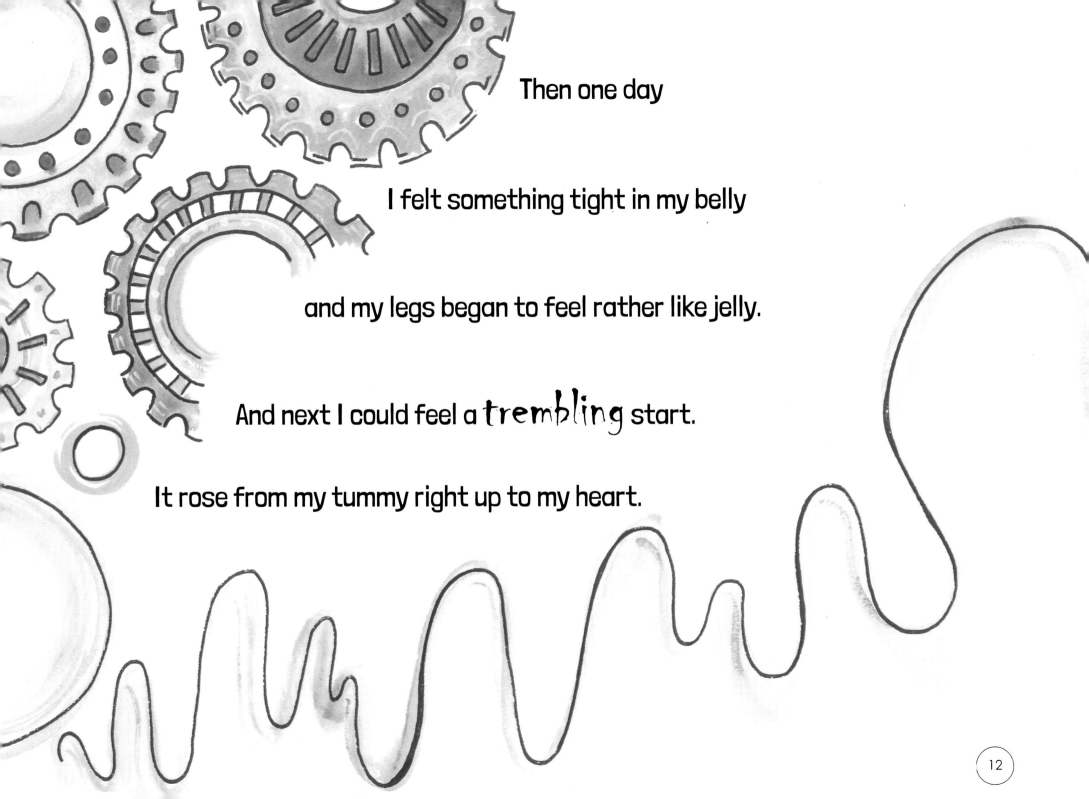

As my heart beat faster,

my face became hot

and I didn't know whether to cry or not.

But my tears seemed to have a plan of their own

as they rolled down my face and I let out a groan.

Then the groan became more like a roar

as my body dropped right down to the floor.

I felt like I was about to drown.

I couldn't look up, I could only look down.

I was really scared I didn't know what to do.

I was shaking so much and felt very sick too.

And then

I felt a hand on my back.

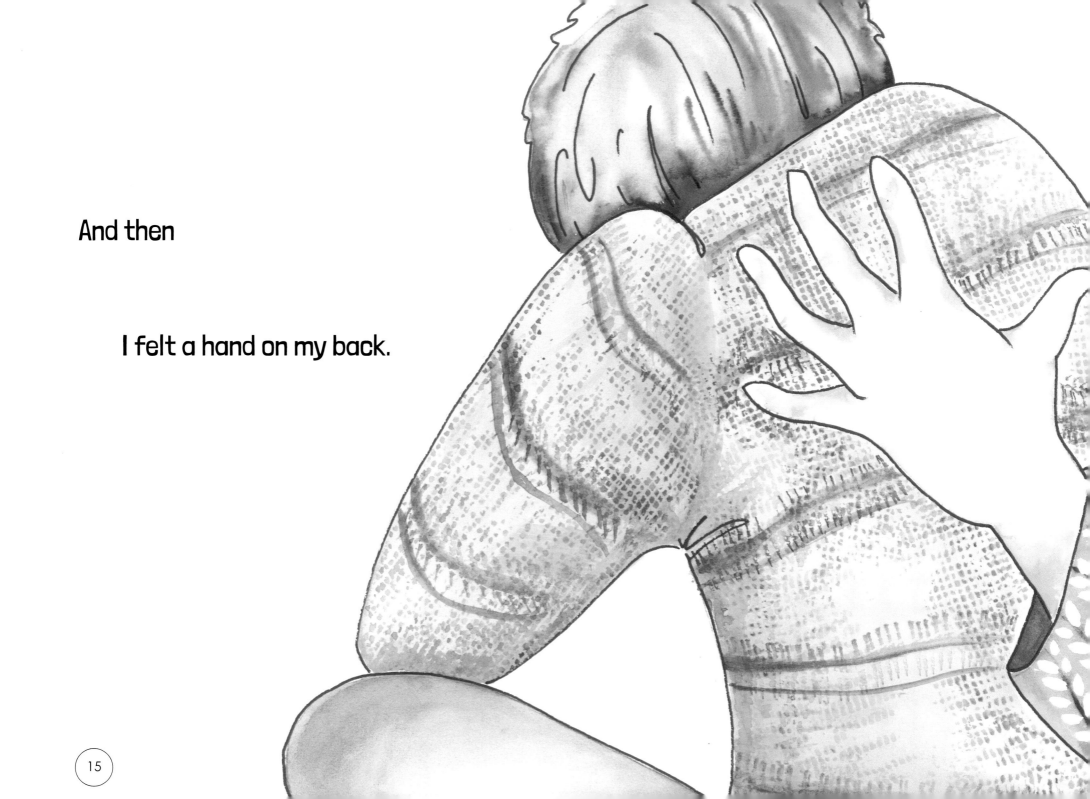

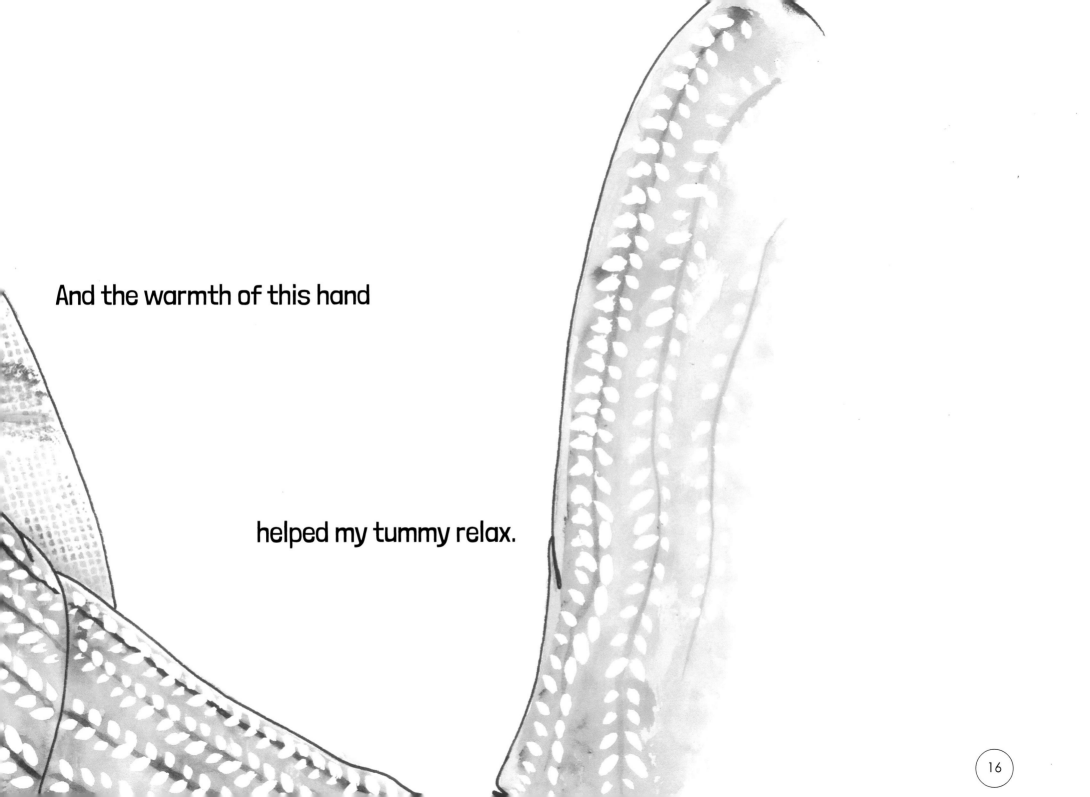

And the warmth of this hand

helped my tummy relax.

There were so many tears they were forming a puddle,

as the hand became arms

that gave me a cuddle.

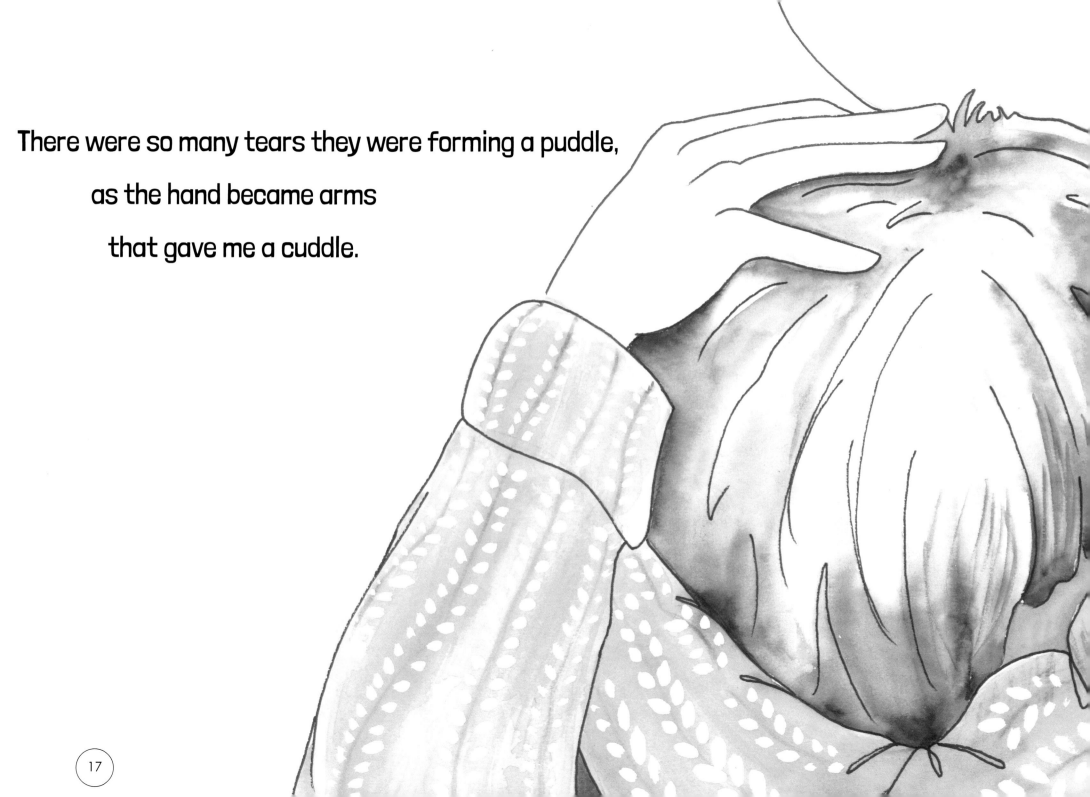

As the arms stayed around me, my head got lighter

and the 'what if?' questions became a little bit quieter.

Now I could feel there was someone here

who could be with me, while I felt this fear.

19

It wasn't answers I needed to all this stuff.

Feeling someone beside me

was simply
enough.

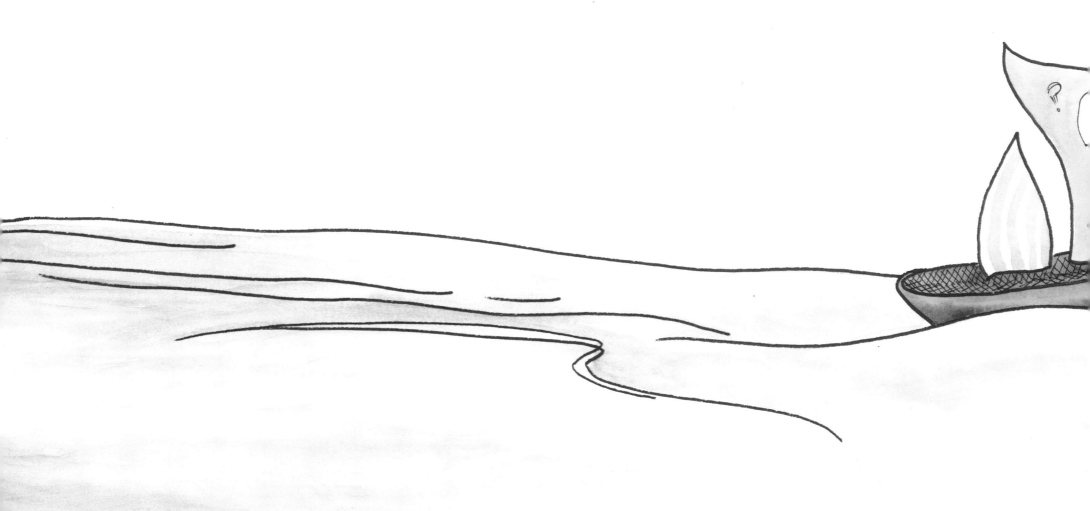

Reflection

How does it feel to be asking all these 'what if' questions?

Do you ever have worry thoughts?

As you reflect on this, notice how it feels in your body:

Does the feeling have a colour?

Does the feeling have a shape?

Does the feeling have a movement?

Does the feeling have a sound?

More reflections, activities and explorations are available in *Being With Our Feelings – A Mindful Approach to Wellbeing for Children: A Teaching Toolkit* by Anita Kate Garai (Routledge, 2022).

Printed in the UK by Severn, Gloucester on responsibly sourced paper

MIX
Paper from
responsible sources
FSC® C022174